Series editor: Lionel Bender

Published by Country Life Books,
an imprint of Newnes Books,
a Division of The Hamlyn Publishing Group Limited
84-88 The Centre, Feltham, Middlesex, England
and distributed for them by The Hamlyn
Publishing Group Limited, Rushden, Northants.

© Newnes Books, a Division of
The Hamlyn Publishing Group Limited 1985

ISBN 0 600 35789 9

Printed in Italy.

THE
COUNTRY LIFE POCKET GUIDE
TO
GARDEN FLOWERS

Peter Blackburne-Maze

COUNTRY LIFE
BOOKS

Contents

Introduction

The aim of this book is to be both a help and an
encouragement to what might be called 'active' as well
as 'passive' gardeners. An active gardener is one who has
a garden to look after and is engaged in practical
gardening. He or she can use the book to help them in
the vital work of planning a complete garden or just for
finding the odd plant to fill a specific need.

A passive gardener is someone who, though interested
in garden plants, is not actually gardening. For such a
person, the book is extremely useful for identifying plants
seen in the normal course of travelling about but whose
name is unknown. To help identification both the
botanical and common names of plants are given. The
inclusion of an index at the end of the book provides yet
another and completely opposite use – that of looking
up a plant by name to see what it looks like.

It would be impossible in a book of this size to include
all the plants that one would like, so coverage is mainly
restricted to those plants most commonly seen in gardens
of northwest Europe and which are readily available in
garden centres, nurseries etc. Even so, over 130 different
plants are illustrated and described fully. In addition,
related species and varieties of sufficient garden merit –
a total of more than 100 – will also be found in the text.

The layout of the book is designed for easy and quick
reference. The main division is into the type of plant –
shrub, herbaceous, water, alpine etc. – so that you can
turn straight to the appropriate section. Within this, the
plants are divided into the season in which they flower.
Finally, there is a rather loose grouping by colour.
Nature being what it is, it is very rare that any plant fits
snugly and firmly into a particular category, especially
where flowering season is concerned. This is catered for
by listing each plant according to the *start* of its flowering
period. However, where flowering spills over from one
period to another, the plant is featured in the text of
the later section as well.

The details and features of each plant are, of necessity,
fairly concise but include all that is needed for either a
broad identification to be carried out or for a gardener
to decide upon the basic suitability of a plant for a
particular purpose. The plant's approximate size is given

– in the case of shrubs, it refers to the size after ten years – together with a more accurate idea of the flowering time. Colours and any recommended varieties and relatives are then given together with, if necessary, the plant's hardiness. Finally will be found any cultural peculiarities or hints on growing the plants successfully.

Azalea, Rhododendron,

Azaleas and rhododendrons make
a grand show in the spring. Their
main colours are red, pink, orange
and yellow but white varieties are
also available. Most are
evergreens.

Rhododendron 'Golden
Oriole' deciduous

Azalea. *Rhododendron*
'Pink Pearl'.

Azaleas are, in fact, a type of *Rhododendron* and are
normally listed as such. There are deciduous and
evergreen species. Their height is usually 1–2m with a
similar spread. Most are woodland plants but they do
not like heavy shade.

The 'true' rhododendrons are evergreen and somewhat
larger, 2m being normal. There are, though, dwarf
species such as *R. impeditum*, which barely reaches 30cm.

Azaleas and rhododendrons require lime-free
conditions if they are to thrive and this often necessitates
plenty of peat being added to the soil at planting time.
In addition, if the young leaves go yellow during the
growing season, apply iron sequestrene early each spring.
Very little pruning is needed apart from shaping, and
this should take place after flowering.

The most popular species of bell heather is *Erica carnea*,
and it is also more tolerant of lime than the others. Its

Erica

Erica carnea
'Myretaun Ruby'.

Erica carnea
'Springwood White'.

Of the winter
flowering *Erica* spp.
E. carnea and its
many varieties are
particularly good as
ground cover. Red,
pink and white are the
predominant colours.

height varies from 15 to 30cm and it spreads well, making
a very good ground cover plant. There are many
varieties, the main difference between them being the
flower colour, but golden foliage ones also exist. They
flower from about February to May. *E. hibernica* is the
tallest species, reaching 1m high. It flowers from January
to May. *E. × darleyensis* will grow to about 30cm and
flowers a month earlier.

Ericas are excellent companions for azaleas and
rhododendrons because they too like acid soil
conditions. Although most ericas will tolerate a certain
amount of lime or chalk in the soil, they rarely thrive;
the ground should contain plenty of peat, with
sequestrene applied in the spring if necessary. The most
important task is clipping the plants after flowering to
remove the old flower heads and to encourage
bushiness; this is best achieved with shears.

Camellia, Magnolia, Syringa

Camellia japonica flowers in late April and May. Camellias have double, semi-double or single flowers in red, pink, white or variously striped.

M. stellata is a smaller magnolia with pure white flowers.

*Magnolia ×
soulangiana* flowers in mid-spring.

Nearly all the camellias that we grow in gardens are varieties or hybrids of *Camellia japonica*. They are evergreen and perfectly hardy but, flowering as they do in April and May, the blooms are sometimes caught by the frost and ruined. They will reach about 1.5m in ten years but older specimens get much bigger.

Especially good varieties include 'Waterlily' (bright pink, double), 'Adolphe Audusson' (red with yellow stamens, semi-double), 'Powder Puff' (white, double) and 'Lady Vansittart' (pink striped with rose, semi-double).

Camellias prefer a lime-free soil amply supplied with organic matter. They should be grown in a warm and sheltered position to protect the flowers from spring frosts and, while appreciating sunshine, they will tolerate semi-shade. Pruning for shape is all that is required.

Magnolias are deciduous shrubs whose flowers appear in April and May before the foliage; as such, they are susceptible to frost damage. Two species are in common

Camellia japonica 'Adolphe Audusson'.

Syringa

Lilac, *Syringa*, makes a large shrub. Many modern hybrids are available in a range of colours from almost red, through pink and lilac, to white. They flower in the spring and are useful for adding height to borders.

cultivation, *Magnolia × soulangiana* and *M. stellata*. *M. × soulangiana* is the larger with a height of 3m. The flowers are spectacular, large and waxy. Apart from the normal colouring, a pure white form exists (*M. × s. alba superba*) as well as one with a redder outside (*M. × s. rubra*). *M. stellata* is about half the size with pure white, many-petalled flowers. The name 'stellata' refers to the flowers' star-like appearance. Lime is tolerated but acid conditions are preferred. Ample organic matter is needed as is a sheltered and warm position to reduce the effects of frost.

Capable of becoming small trees, lilacs (*Syringa* spp.) are seen in a great variety of colours and with flowers either single or double. Flowering lasts for about three weeks and covers the period mid-May to early June. The height of the shrub can vary from 1.5–3m according to the variety. Lilacs dislike heavy shade but otherwise are tolerant of a wide range of conditions.

13

Berberis, Philadelphus, Forsythia

Forsythia × 'Lynwood'.

Berberis × stenophylla is one of the most decorative of the family. It is evergreen with yellow flowers in the spring.

Good species of *Berberis* (barberry) include *B. wilsoniae* (deciduous, good autumn colour with coral-pink berries), *B. thunbergii atropurpurea* (deciduous, purple leaves), *B. darwinii* (evergreen, glossy green leaves, smaller). All *Berberis* have thorny shoots and/or leaves and specimen bushes need little or no pruning.

Although *B. × stenophylla* makes a good shrub, its main use is as an informal hedge, where its evergreen leaves and bright orange, scented flowers in April and May brighten any garden. Pruning should be done after flowering and consist of removing the longest shoots that have flowered to prevent the hedge spreading too far.

The flowers of all *Philadelphus* (mock orange) varieties are produced in great abundance and many have a delicious scent; some people think that it is rather too strong. Besides 'Belle Etoile' and 'Virginal', there is a lovely variety *P. coronarius aureus* that has bright yellow

Philadelphus 'Belle Etoile' is somewhat smaller than the more common 'Virginal' and is more fragrant. Both are indispensable spring-flowering shrubs, the choice depending on the available room.

Philadelphus 'Belle Etoile'.

Forsythia × 'Lynwood' is one of our most popular April-flowering shrubs and is good for cutting for the house. The more vigorous *F. suspensa* is perfect for training against a wall.

leaves early in the growing season.

The shrubs should be pruned by cutting out any branches that have become old and worn out or simply out-of-place. This should be done straight after flowering to give maximum time for new shoots to grow. A sunny position suits the plants best but semi-shade is tolerable.

One of the most startling sights in April are the golden yellow bushes of *Forsythia*. The more upright of the two common species, *F. intermedia*, is sometimes grown as a hedge, but the hard clipping necessary makes it quite unsuitable as most of the flowering shoots are removed in the process. Pruning should take place in May, removing worn out branches to encourage new ones to grow. *F. suspensa* has a far more weeping habit and is best trained against a wall or shed so that the long, arching shoots can develop to the full. Both species are deciduous.

Deutzia, Escallonia, Fuchsia

Deutzia × 'Mont Rose'.

Deutzia × 'Mont Rose' is altogether a finer shrub than the more common *D. scabra*; it has larger and more open flowers which are mauve/pink instead of white.

Although not a common shrub, *Deutzia* is well worth growing as it is reliable and full of flowers. It is deciduous and flowers during June and July. An attractive feature is the peeling bark. The young shoots are apt to be tender and may be damaged by spring frosts.

'Mont Rose' does not make a large shrub, 1.8m being about normal. After flowering, prune the oldest shoots hard back to make room for more. Deutzias are quite happy on most soil types.

Escallonia is a valuable summer flowering shrub that also makes an excellent informal hedge. Most species are about 1.8m high with a similar spread. Many hybrids exist, some of the best being 'C. F. Ball' (crimson flowers), 'Donard Radiance' (bright pink), 'Slieve Donard' (pale pink, hardy) and 'Iveyi' (white, vigorous). All have aromatic leaves.

Unfortunately, escallonias are only reliably hardy in

Escallonia Donard Seedling makes a particularly attractive evergreen shrub with pale pink flowers.

Although fuchsias are some of the most popular greenhouse and bedding plants, some species, such as *F. magellanica variegata*, make good border plants with their dainty, hanging flowers appearing throughout the summer and autumn.

milder districts but they can be protected with polythene sheeting on the coldest nights. In warm areas they are likely to be evergreen but in colder districts they may lose some leaves, though growing them against a wall or house usually prevents this.

Of those species of *Fuchsia* suitable for the garden, varieties of *F. magellanica* are among the hardiest, with *F.m. riccartonii* being the sturdiest of all. Others that will survive outdoors include 'Madame Cornellisen' (scarlet sepals, white within), 'Mrs. Popple' (carmine and violet), 'Tom Thumb' (carmine and violet) and 'Versicolor' (crimson purple).

Fuchsias are not normally regarded as being hardy enough to grow outdoors all the year round but several species are quite strong enough, though they are usually killed to the ground each winter. Pruning consists of cutting all shoots down to the ground in the early spring.

17

Weigela, Cistus, Hydrangea,

Weigela 'Bristol Ruby' is one of the finest of the family and a particularly good summer-flowering shrub for small gardens.

Ceanothus are especially valuable because they are some of the few shrubs that have reliably blue flowers. *C. thyrsiflorus* is an evergreen that flowers in May and June. It succeeds best against a wall.

Most weigelas will grow to about 2m so are suitable for all but the smallest gardens. Although true species are sometimes grown, most of those in gardens are hybrids. They flower during May and June.

Besides 'Bristol Ruby', other good varieties are 'Abel Carriere' (rosy carmine with yellow throat) and 'Newport Red' (bright red, dark red foliage). They are best pruned by removing the oldest branches after flowering. On very chalky soils, they may need an application of sequestrene to maintain good leaf colour.

Cistus are excellent small (less than 2m) evergreen shrubs that flower continuously from late May till nearly August in a wide range of generally pastel shades. Unfortunately, they are unreliably hardy.

The 'mop head' *Hydrangea macrophylla* (Hortensia) is the most commonly seen species of the genus, with its large flower heads appearing from July to September.

Ceanothus

Hydrangea macrophylla is the most common member of a large family. The spectacular flower-heads are usually pink but, under acid conditions, may be a glorious blue.

The pink paper flowers of *Cistus* 'Peggy Sannons' give a long succession of colour through the summer.

The usual height is about 1.5m.

The dead flowers should be left until after the winter to give protection to the slightly tender shoots. In March, the shoots are removed along with any elderly branches so that the shrub is kept young. Never shorten back long shoots as this removes the flower buds.

Another attractive hydrangea is the 'Lace Cap', in which only the outside flowers of the head have petals. The 'climbing hydrangea' *H. petiolaris*, is a true climber and is particularly valuable for planting against a north facing wall. It has white flower heads in June.

Although most *Ceanothus* are hardy, the evergreen species succeed best in a warm and protected position. Among these, *C. thyrsiflorus* produces bright blue flower heads in May and any pruning for shape should take place after that. Other good varieties are 'Gloire de Versailles' and 'Topaz' (see page 26).

Potentilla, Cytisus, Hypericum,

Cytisus × praecox, Warminster broom, is one of the best cultivated forms of our wild broom. It flowers in May and, with age, develops a weeping habit.

The low-growing *Potentilla fruticosa* 'Tangerine' is a hardy but deciduous ground-cover plant that will flower all summer. Yellow and red varieties are available.

All the potentillas are small, colourful shrubs growing, on average, to 1m high. Good varieties of *Potentilla fruticosa* include 'Abbotswood' (white, greyish foliage), 'Katherine Dykes' (yellow), 'Red Ace' (flame), 'Royal Flush' (dark pink) and 'Princess' (pale pink). They are completely hardy and prefer a sunny position to give of their best. Many will remain in flower from May until October. Lightly clipping them in early spring is the best way of keeping them in shape.

Cytisus × praecox is just one example of the many broom plants that are grown quite easily in gardens. It reaches about 1.2m with a similar spread. A white flowered form, 'Albus', also exists.

Possibly more widely grown are the varieties of *C. scoparius*, whose flowers may be multi- or single-coloured. All are around 1.5m high. Pruning should be done after flowering to stop seed pods forming and weakening the plant, but large branches must be cut out

Senecio

The glory of *Senecio* 'Sunshine' lies in its grey, evergreen leaves. During summer these contrast beautifully with the bright yellow flowers.

Hypericum patulum 'Hidcote' is one of the best of the shrubby varieties. Its numerous golden flowers almost hide the foliage during the late summer.

with caution as brooms tend not to send out fresh shoots from older wood.

Several hypericums are first-rate garden shrubs. Besides *Hypericum patulum* 'Hidcote', *H. inodorum* 'Elstead' is worth noting. It has smaller flowers than Hidcote but these are followed by bright orange-scarlet berries. At 1m tall, it is also slightly smaller. A variegated variety, 'Tricolor', is about the same size but has pink, green and cream leaves. The low growing *H. calycinum* (Rose of Sharon) is a vigorous ground cover plant that should be clipped close to the ground in early spring about one year in three.

One of the most popular shrubs with grey foliage is *Senecio laxifolius*. Although the upper surface of the leaves is approaching green, the underside is almost white. Bright yellow daisy-like flowers are produced in June and July. Fairly drastic pruning is sometimes needed in the early spring to prevent the bushes becoming leggy.

Rosa – the rose family

Floribundas are grown for their mass-colour effect rather than their individual flowers and start flowering earlier than the hybrid teas.

'All gold'

'Pascali'

Hybrid teas are the most popular roses and rely on the beauty of the individual flowers that are borne, largely singly, on the end of the current season's shoots.

'Just Joey'

'Peace'

Well-tended bushes of hybrid tea and floribunda roses can provide flowers from June right through until the autumn frosts finally put a stop to growth. Both are best grown in formal settings with several bushes of each variety. Colours vary from dark red through all shades of red, pink and yellow to white. Fairly hard pruning is needed to maintain the bushes in good shape and this should begin in November, when the shoots are cut back by about half. Follow up in March by harder pruning.

The climbing varieties are normally grown against walls and fences or simply against wires to support them in the open garden. They are best tied in periodically during the summer to prevent them being blown about, but this may be left until the autumn, when they also are headed back. Proper pruning follows in March.

Rambler roses are also trained to some form of support

True rose species are either naturally occurring or are improved versions of these. They have attractive flowers which are often followed by colourful hips in the autumn.

Climbing roses, such as 'Mermaid', have a permanent framework of stiff stems. Flowers are large, solitary or in clusters. Unlike rambler roses, there is little new growth from the base of the plant.

'Mermaid'

and tend to concentrate their flowering into a shorter period during the summer. This must be followed by cutting back to the ground most of the flowered growths to give plenty of time for next year's flowering shoots to develop.

Shrub roses of the *Rosa rugosa* type are less formal and are often used very effectively as flowering hedges. In such cases, little pruning is needed beyond keeping the bushes in bounds and removing any remaining hips in March.

The true and improved species of roses can be treated as normal shrubs as regards placing and pruning. They have a great variety of flower sizes and colours but it is really their hips in the autumn that give them their garden value. *R. moyesii* 'Geranium' is especially good.

Roses appreciate a sunny position but are not particular to the soil type providing it is well drained.

23

Buddleia, Spiraea, Hebe, Vinca

Hebe pinguifolia 'Pagei' is a low-growing evergreen shrub with small leaves and many heads of white flowers in early summer.

Buddleia davidii is often called the butterfly bush as its fragrant flowers have a great attraction for the insects. There are many varieties of different flower colours.

The wide colour range of *Buddleia* spp. now available make them very popular garden shrubs. All the *B. davidii* varieties are vigorous and flower from July to September. They soon attain a height of 3m.

B. globosa carries small, round, orange flower heads in the spring. It needs to be pruned only for shape but other species should be pruned hard in the early spring by cutting the long flowering shoots back to the older wood.

Of the several *Spiraea* grown in gardens, 'Anthony Waterer' is one of the most popular. It reaches about 90cm in height and produces its dark red flower heads from July to September. Another good one is the larger *S. × arguta* (Bridal Wreath, foam of May), whose long, arching stems are covered with small white flowers during April and May.

Vinca minor, the lesser periwinkle, is a better and less invasive species than *V. major*. It is a splendid ground-cover plant and has delightful blue flowers during the summer.

Spiraea 'Anthony Waterer' is a small shrub that flowers in the summer but whose main feature is the variegated leaves.

Any pruning should be done in the early spring to keep the bushes young.

Hebe pinguifolia 'Pagei' is a particularly useful low-growing shrub for rockeries, where the grey, evergreen leaves contrast well with darker plants. It seldom reaches more than 30cm high but spreads to nearly 90cm and, if the plant becomes leggy with age, can be pruned back hard in April.

Vinca minor (the Lesser Periwinkle) is neater in every respect than *V. major* and is far more suitable for gardens. There is also a variegated form. Both carry purple flowers that come out mainly in May, but with 'Bowles' Variety', they are blue and appear from July to August. See also *V. major*, page 28.

Ceanothus, Hebe

Ceanothus 'Gloire de Versailles' flowers from July to October with pale blue flowers. It is deciduous shrub with a weeping habit.

Of the *Ceanothus* that flower from July to October, 'Gloire de Versailles' has pale blue flower heads, an almost weeping habit and reaches 1.8m high with a similar spread. 'Topaz' is slightly smaller and more compact, with brighter blue flowers. Both are deciduous, hardier than the evergreen varieties (see page 19) and will grow quite happily in the north of England in a sheltered position. They will flower at their best when pruned back hard to the old wood in April once there are signs of growth.

Hebe 'Autumn Glory' is an evergreen shrub with dark, glossy leaves tinged with purple and heads of charming violet-blue flowers carried from June to October.

Hebe 'Great Orme' is a late flowering shrub with spikes of pink flowers.

The later-flowering *Hebes* (formerly the shrubby veronicas) cover the period from midsummer almost until the frosts. Most are about 1m high and some of the best include *H. anomala* (yellow-green foliage, white flower heads), 'Autumn Glory' (purple-tinged leaves, violet blue), 'Great Orme' (pink), 'Marjorie' (pale violet and white, very hardy) and *H. speciosa* 'La Seduisante' (bright crimson). All are evergreens and normally hardy but may be damaged in a severe winter. They like a well-drained soil and flower best in a sunny position. Pruning is usually restricted to keeping the bushes shapely but if they are killed back during the winter they can be cut back hard in April with every chance that they will grow out again.

It should also be remembered that the hardy fuchsias (see page 17) will flower well into the autumn. Most will continue until spoilt by the frost.

27

Calluna, Vinca

Probably the best form of the periwinkle is *Vinca major variegata*. It is invasive but the variegated leaves make an attractive ground cover in the winter.

The golden foliage of *Calluna vulgaris* 'Gold Haze' is evergreen. White flowers are produced in August and September.

Wild heather (ling) is at its best in August and September. Many varieties exist; some of the best are: *Calluna vulgaris* 'My Dream' (double white), 'H. E. Beale' (double pink), 'Gold Haze' (golden foliage, white), 'Silver Knight' (silvery foliage, white) and 'Wickwar Flame' (orange to red foliage, lavender). All varieties must have acid soil conditions but on limey or chalky land they can quite easily be grown by building up a bed of peat on top of the normal soil. As with *Erica*, they should be clipped after flowering to induce bushiness and prevent straggly growth.

Of the several periwinkles, the most commonly seen is *Vinca major*. This is a vigorous growing plant that sends out long stems over the ground that need constant cutting back to stop them smothering more valuable plants. The variegated form is slightly weaker and therefore easier to manage. See also *V. minor*, page 25.

28

Erica, Daphne

Erica × darleyensis starts flowering in November and carries on until April. The flowers are pink but there is a pure white form and another with golden foliage.

Daphne mezereum is a favourite winter-flowering shrub. The pinky lilac flowers are borne on leafless stems right through the winter.

Erica × darleyensis varieties are some of the best winter-flowering heathers. The true species is among the earliest to flower along with its varieties 'J. H. Brummage' (golden foliage) and 'Silver Beads' (pure white flowers), while 'A. T. Johnson' (light green foliage, magenta) starts a little later in December. Acid soils are preferred but slightly alkaline conditions are tolerated.

These make excellent ground-cover plants for keeping the weeds down among other shrubs or they can be grown in beds on their own or in company with small conifers.

Daphne mezereum, or the mezereon, is an easy-to-grow shrub that is often seen flowering from February until April, when the leaves appear. It seldom grows more than 1.2m high and has an upright habit. The flowers are usually a pale lilac but a white form also exists. Both are strongly scented. They will grow in most soil types and are quite at home in semi-shade.

Viburnum, Hamamelis, Chimonanthus

Viburnum × bodnantense 'Dawn' is the best of the winter-flowering viburnums. The clusters of pink and white flowers start to appear in November and keep going right through the winter.

Probably the most popular and best known winter-flowering shrub is *Viburnum farreri* (formerly *V. fragrans*). The white clusters of sweetly scented flowers tinged with pink appear as early as November and continue well into March. The normal height of the plant is about 1.5m and the growth is upright with spreading branches. *V. × bodnantense* 'Dawn' is similarly sized but has larger individual flowers in bigger clusters.

Another winter-flowering viburnum is the evergreen *V. tinus (Laurustinus).* This is some 3m high and more spreading. The pinkish-white flowers appear from late November until maybe April and are often followed by metallic blue berries.

Witch hazel has long been a favourite shrub. The one normally seen is *Hamamelis mollis*, which carries beautifully scented yellow flowers, red at the centre, on the leafless branches from December to March. It grows to 2m high and, if necessary, should be pruned after

Chimonanthus praecox 'Luteus' is a treasure but not very hardy. The flowers have a delicious scent, are pale yellow and appear from November to March.

Another winter favourite is the witch hazel. *Hamamelis × intermedia* 'Jelena' is an improved form having petals which are pink at the base and lemon yellow at the tips. The flowers are fragrant.

flowering to keep its shape, which can become rather straggly. The variety 'Pallida' has pure yellow flowers. *H. × intermedia* varieties are hybrids of *H. mollis* and *H. japonica* and include 'Jelena', 'Magic Fire' and 'Moonlight'.

Chimonanthus praecox 'Luteus', the winter sweet, is another outstanding shrub with a delightful scent, but is not quite as hardy as the witch hazel. It grows to 2m.

'Grandiflorus' has flowers that are deeper yellow than the type and with a reddish stain at the centre. It is somewhat earlier flowering than 'Luteus'.

Any deeply cultivated soil will suit winter sweet but it is always better in a warm and sunny position, preferably against a wall. No pruning is necessary beyond the removal of any frosted shoots in April once growth has started.

31

Clematis

Some of the finest spring-flowering
climbers are the *Clematis* species. *C. alpina*
has light blue flowers during April and
May.

Clematis are among the best of spring-flowering climbers.
Besides the familiar *C. montana*, stems 6–9m long,
whose pink or white flowers appear in May and June,
many less common species are grown quite easily,
among them the pale blue *C. alpina*, 2–3m.

Another blue species is *C. macropetala*, which will grow
a little larger; it flowers during April and May.

All these early species should, if necessary, be pruned
after flowering when dead shoots and any that are
getting too vigorous are cut out.

All *Clematis* will need support and, besides using the
vigorous varieties for covering an unsightly shed or wall,
one of the nicest ways is to train them up into a tree.
Laburnum is a good 'host' as it flowers at the same time.

There are no special soil needs but *Clematis* succeed
best when well supplied with lime and organic matter.

Clematis

Clematis × 'Ernest Markham'.

The pride of the summer climbers must surely be the *Clematis* hybrids such as *C.* × 'Jackmanii' and 'Ernest Markham'. The range of colours varies from every shade of blue, purple and pink as well as white.

Clematis × 'Jackmanii'

Of the many fine *Clematis* hybrids, most originate from the Lanuginosa, Jackmanii and Viticella groups.

Besides 'Jackmanii' and 'Ernest Markham', some of the best large flowered varieties are 'Nelly Moser' (almost white with red stripe in the centre of the petals), 'Lasurstern' (blue), 'Madame le Coultre' (white) and 'Mrs. Thompson' (dark lilac with deep red stripe).

Although quite vigorous, they are not especially strong and average 3–6m in height. The best flowers and neatest habit are obtained when the plants are cut back hard to within 30cm of the ground before the end of February. This delays flowering until later summer; for early flowers, cut back after the first flush is over.

Lonicera, Wisteria

No garden is complete without the scent of honeysuckle, *Lonicera periclymenum*, from June onwards. Most are vigorous climbers so need plenty of room. Not all are scented.

One of the finest climbers of all is *Wisteria sinensis* with its charming racemes of lilac/blue flowers that appear in May. It is, though, even more rampant than honeysuckle.

Honeysuckles' vigour will vary with the species and variety. Strong growing sorts like *Lonicera periclymenum* will soon reach a spread of 6–9m but neater ones may spread only 4m. *L. periclymenum* is deciduous but 'Dropmore Scarlet', along with *L. japonica* 'Halliana', will retain most of its leaves in winter.

Not all varieties of honeysuckle are scented; *L. × tellmanniana*, for example, is not at all. The flowering period varies as well. *L. periclymenum* flowers during June whereas 'Halliana' lasts from July to October.

Probably the most spectacular sight during May and June is *Wisteria sinensis*. The pendulous clusters of pale lilac-blue flowers can almost cover a shed or wall, up which this very vigorous climber should be grown. Although most soils are suitable, wisterias should always be grown in the sun. Prune the strong young shoots back in July and again in winter.

Polygonum

Mile-a-minute or the Russian vine, *Polygonum baldschuanicum*, is the most vigorous and energetic of climbers. It is perfect for covering ugly sheds, etc. It is deciduous and has attractive heads of white flowers in the autumn.

Once the Russian vine *Polygonum baldschuanicum* has been seen, its indomitable vigour is seldom forgotten. It is the strongest climber we have and as such needs careful siting if it is not to become a nuisance. When grown up a dead or unwanted tree, the effect in late summer and autumn, when it is in flower, can be quite spectacular, giving the impression of a waterfall with weeping flower shoots tumbling down. Pruning is virtually impossible and indeed unnecessary if it has been planted in a suitable place where it can be allowed to grow freely.

With all climbers of this vigour, it must be remembered that tiles and slates on shed roofs over which the vine is growing can very easily be lifted without you being aware of the damage.

35

Jasminum

The winter jasmine,
Jasminum nudiflorum,
brightens winter days from
November onwards. The
primrose-yellow flowers,
carried on the leafless
shoots, are often damaged
by sharp frost.

Very few climbers flower during the winter but
undoubtedly the finest is the winter jasmine *Jasminum
nudiflorum*. It can be relied upon to provide a wealth of
flowers from November right through until early March.

This is not a self-clinging climber and has to be trained
and tied in place. The best specimens are seen where
the plants are protected from the early morning sun, as
quick thawing of the frosted flowers will soon ruin them.
In addition, they will have been pruned hard back to the
old wood each year after flowering to encourage the
production of many vigorous young shoots for flowering
the following winter.

Nymphaea, Caltha

The most colourful of pond plants is the waterlily, *Nymphaea* spp. The wavy flowers of the wild species are yellow but this plant is too vigorous in pools so the smaller red-, pink- and white-flowered are preferred.

The marsh marigold, *Caltha palustris* 'Flore Pleno', is one of the earliest plants to flower in the water garden. Its rich golden flowers open in the early spring and it is often seen adorning the shallow margin of pools.

Our native waterlily *Nymphaea alba* is too vigorous for small pools. Where suitable, though, its variety 'Gladstoniana' has larger flowers and is one of the best whites. *N. caroliniana nivea* is much neater and has many large white flowers.

Of the smaller varieties, 'Aurora' has bright yellow flowers, with green and red variegated leaves; 'Turicensis' has soft pink flowers with a sweet scent and 'Froebeli' has wine-red flowers.

Most waterlilies grow best in water from 20–60cm deep and each plant will cover a surface area of 0.1–0.7m².

Although more of a bogplant than a true water one, the marsh marigold *Caltha palustris* and its varieties are indispensible around pools. They flower from March to May. The variety 'Flore Plena' has fully double flowers and is best for gardens; 'Alba' has white flowers.

37

Hyacinthus, Narcissus

Although one usually associates *Narcissus* with the short trumpeted varieties such as 'Rockall', it also covers all the daffodils. Apart from the large cut-flower varieties, there is an enormous number of smaller ones and miniatures. *N. bulbocodium* and *N. cyclamineus* are two of the best of the latter; both are delightful rockery plants.

The hyacinth, *Hyacinthus* spp., is excellent as both a bedding plant and an indoor pot plant. The flowers are scented and are available in white and shades of red, pink, yellow, blue and purple.

Narcissus 'Rockall'

Because of its relatively high price per bulb, the hyacinth (*Hyacinthus* spp.) is more usually grown in bowls for indoor decoration. It is, however, one of the finest spring bedding plants for small borders, where its wide range of colours suit it perfectly for planting with other low-growing plants like the Siberian wallflower and forget-me-not.

Outdoors hyacinths seldom reach 30cm high. Popular varieties include 'Gypsy Queen' (buff orange), 'Jan Bos' (crimson), 'L'innocence' (white), 'Delft Blue', 'Pink Pearl' and 'Yellow Hammer'.

If the bulbs have to be lifted before the foliage has died down, to make room for other plants, they should be replanted somewhere else until the leaves are turning yellow.

The ever-popular daffodil is certainly the best known of all the *Narcissus* species and it exists in many dozens of different forms, from the bright golden 'King Alfred'

Narcissus cyclamineus

Narcissus bulbocodium

to 'Mount Hood' with its white petals and very pale
yellow trumpet. There are also many varieties of what we
normally call 'narcissi'. 'Geranium' is popular, with
white petals and a small, bright orange cup. It has one
flower per stem whereas 'Cheerfulness' has up to four.
These are sweetly scented and cream coloured. Most
flower from March onward.

Among the miniatures, possibly the most widely grown
is 'Angel's Tears'. It barely reaches 10cm high and has
almost pure white flowers. The hoop petticoat narcissus,
N. bulbocodium, is about the same size and flowers in
February/March. It has tiny golden petals but a large
trumpet.

When grown in borders, narcissi flower best if lifted,
split up and replanted every three or four years. Many
of the miniatures are seen in rockeries but one of the
nicest ways of growing all narcissi is to allow them to
spread naturally in grass.

Crocus, Iris, Tulipa, Scilla

Iris reticulata

Iris danfordiae

One of the first *Crocus* to flower in the early spring is *C. tomasinianus*. Its pale lavender flowers frequently appear before all the snow has gone.

There are two particularly good dwarf bulbous irises, both of which flower early. Though a pale blue variety of *Iris reticulata* exists, purple is the normal colour. *I. danfordiae* is smaller and earlier with bright yellow flowers.

By the end of February, we may well be seeing the first of the spring crocuses, *Crocus* spp., coming into flower. These are the ones that occur naturally in different parts of Europe. Among the earliest is *C. tomasinianus*, whose scented, greyish-lavender flowers are freely produced. 'Cloth of Gold' is another early crocus, with bright orange flowers streaked with brown. A little later comes *C. versicolor picturatus*, with white flowers finely marked with purple.

Often appearing early in February, the dwarf bulbous *Iris danfordiae* is usually seen planted in rockeries. Its bright yellow flowers are scarcely 5cm off the ground and these are followed by the 30cm-high stalk-like leaves. Coming a few weeks later is its better-known relation *I. reticulata*, with normally a rich blue, almost purple, flower, but pale blue and even white forms exist. The petals are narrower than those of *I. danfordiae* and stand some 10cm tall. Both flower best in full sun and in a dry

Scilla sibirica is a charming rockery plant with dainty bright blue bell-like flowers in March.

Tulips represent probably the largest family of spring-flowering bulbs, including the parrot tulip (above) and *Tulipa praestans* shown left.

position where the bulbs can get baked in the summer sunshine.

Although the smaller *Tulipa* species are often planted informally, for example *T. kaufmanniana* (the waterlily tulip) and *T. praestans* (red), the majority are much larger and showier and are used for spring-bedding displays. The range of colours is seemingly endless, as is their height variation. The Darwin tulips are the most widely seen. These are up to 60cm high and blend particularly well with wallflowers. Other types that are often grown include lily flowered, cottage, Rembrandt (streaked flowers) and parrot tulips.

The *Scilla* is one of the daintiest little spring flowers; almost like a miniature bluebell with four or five flowers per stem. These are an intense blue colour. The species usually seen is *S. sibirica*, which has dark blue, light blue and white varieties. As they usually set seed, a clump will quickly spread.

Cyclamen, Galanthus, Muscari

Cyclamen coum is a perfectly easily grown and delightful little flower that looks particularly at home around the base of a tree. Other spring-flowering species include *C. libanoticum* and *C. repandum*.

As well as being one of the earliest spring-flowering bulbs, the snowdrop, *Galanthus nivalis*, is also among the easiest to grow and, when naturalized in grass, will increase year by year.

Cyclamen coum is the most frequently seem wild cyclamen species. It has pink flowers appearing in February and March; there is also a white variety. Both have plain leaves. *C. libanoticum* is a little later, has similar flowers but beautifully marbled leaves, and is only marginally hardy. *C. repandum* comes in April with pink flowers and toothed, marbled leaves.

Although not the easiest of plants to grow, they are certainly one of the prettiest and there are many to choose from. Most are well suited to rockery conditions but growing naturally among grass is possibly their best position.

The snowdrop is probably the flower that, more than any other, heralds the spring. Its nodding white flowers often come in January when the snow is still thick on the ground. They usually last for a month, or even more. *Galanthus nivalis* is the true snowdrop but it is sometimes

A very popular spring bulb is the grape hyacinth. *Muscari armeniacum* is the normal blue species but a white one, *M. botryoides album*, is also commonly seen. They look best when grown in grass where their dying leaves are soon hidden.

Muscari armeniacum

Muscari botryoides album.

confused with the May-flowering snowflake, *Leucojum vernum*, which is a taller plant with 15cm-tall flower stems. Unlike most other bulbs, the time to move snowdrops is after flowering when they are still growing strongly.

The grape hyacinth, *Muscari armeniacum*, is often seen growing in cottage gardens where it is frequently left alone and allowed to spread at will. It gets its name from the appearance of the flower-heads; similar to an upside-down bunch of grapes. The normal colour is bright blue; *M. botryoides album* is pure white and well worth growing with the blue. Both are about 15cm in height and flower in April. Unfortunately, the leaves are rather untidy as they tend to flop to the ground soon after emergence, which gives the plants a somewhat bedraggled look.

Acidanthera, Ornithogalum, Gladiolus

Closely related to the gladiolus, *Acidanthera bicolor* differs by having a charming scent. The large, white, autumn flowers have a deep-purple throat.

Ornithogalum nutans is another charming plant that will increase rapidly by seeding itself. The flowers are green on the outside and white within and are produced in April/May.

A very pleasing bulb and one not seen as often as it deserves to be, *Acidanthera bicolor murielae* is a greatly improved form of the original *A. bicolor*. It flowers late in the summer and into the autumn producing a spike of sweetly scented flowers and growing 60–90cm high. The bulbs are not completely hardy and should be lifted and stored each autumn and replanted in the spring. *Acidanthera* succeeds best in a warm and sunny position.

Flowering in the spring and early summer, *Ornithogalum umbellatum*, Star of Bethlehem, is an excellent plant for brightening up a dull corner with its 15–22cm-high white flower-heads. An even better known species, *O. thyrsoides*, the chincherinchee, is June-flowering, taller and white to golden in colour. It is not as hardy as *O. umbellatum* and needs a warm site to succeed.

The most popular and widely grown summer flowering

Gladiolus byzantinus

Gladiolus hybrids

Although the gladiolus is one of the best-known summer flowers, it is normally the large flowered hybrids that are grown. In many respects even nicer are the smaller *Gladiolus primulinus* and Butterfly varieties. The trumpet-shaped flowers come in a wide range of colours and bicolours.

bulb is certainly the gladiolus. Its tall flower spikes, up to 1.2m high, are seen in many gardens and often appear in flower shows vying for prizes. The large-flowered *Gladiolus* hybrids are the most frequently grown and can be a spectacular sight when grown in large clumps towards the back of mixed borders where the other plants give them shelter and hide the rather uninteresting stems.

Not so tall and with smaller individual flowers are the Primulinus hybrids and the butterfly gladioli. These are daintier plants, often with a greater contrast between the throat colour and that of the petals.

Though they are safe to leave in the ground over the winter in mild areas, it is normal to lift and store all gladioli.

A hardier species is *G. byzantinus* from Turkey. This may be left outside where it will produce wine-red flowers in June and July. It grows to about 60cm tall.

45

Lilium

L. tigrinum

L. regale

Most lilies are sufficiently hardy to be left in the ground all year round. Their height varies somewhat but it is usually in the range of 1.2 to 1.5m.

Among the most easily grown are *Lilium candidum* (Madonna lily; normally pure white, flowering in June), *L. chalcedonicum* (bright scarlet, July), *L. hansonii* (orange yellow, June/July), *L. martagon* (Turk's cap lily, purplish red, June/July), *L. regale* (regal lily, white with purplish outside, July) and *L. tigrinum* (Tiger lily, orange, spotted, August/September). All these are tolerant of chalky soil.

46

L. auratum

L. martagon

L. candidum

Lilium, lily species, are much easier to grow than is generally thought and they are among the prettiest and most interesting summer bulbs. All the following do well in most gardens. *L. tigrinum*, tiger lily, *L. martagon*, Turk's cap lily, *L. candidum*, madonna lily, *L. auratum*, golden-rayed lily, and *L. regale*, regal lily.

Some species form roots on the underground part of the stem as well as the base of the bulb; these are best planted 7–8cm deep. In this group are *L. formosanum*, *Hansonii*, *henryi*, *regale*, *speciosum* and *tigrinum*.

Those species that only root from the bulb should be planted 15cm deep. These include *L. canadense*, *candidum*, *martagon* and *pardalinum*.

Lilies give of their best when in a position that is not in the blazing sun, so are well suited to growing in herbaceous or shrub borders. The soil should be well supplied with bulky organic matter.

Colchicum, Crocus, Cyclamen, Nerine

Colchicum autumnale is often known as the autumn crocus but its true name is the meadow saffron. Its lilac flowers appear in autumn after the leaves have died down. White, double white and double lilac varieties are also grown.

Crocus speciosus has lavender flowers veined and speckled darker with a white or pale lilac throat.

Colchicum autumnale is the best known and most widely grown of the 'autumn crocuses'. It flowers in August and usually grows 10cm high. Other Colchicum species include C. byzantinum (rose lilac with green dots, August), C. sibthorpii (red purple, large, patterned, September-October) and C. speciosum and its varieties. Many hybrids exist as well.

There are also some true Crocus species that flower in the autumn. C. speciosus is possibly the most often grown; its flowers are various shades of lavender. Others include C. sativus (rosy lilac), C. pulchellus 'Zephyr' (white shaded with grey), C. ochroleucus (cream with orange throat) and C. medius (bright purple).

The wild cyclamen are some of the prettiest of our autumn-flowering bulbs. Cyclamen europaeum comes into flower in August (crimson, scented, plain or marbled foliage), but probably the most popular is C.

Of the autumn-flowering wild cyclamen, *C. neapolitanum* is the most widely grown and looks particularly attractive around the base of trees with its nodding pink flowers and beautifully marbled leaves.

Nerine bowdenii, the Guernsey lily, looks far too exotic to be as easy to grow as it is. The deeply reflexed pink flower-heads appear in the early autumn.

neapolitanum (rose, sometimes scented, very marbled leaves). It flowers from September to November and a white variety is also grown. Although the general appearance of wild cyclamen is similar to that of the well-known pot plant, they are only a fraction of the size and are hardy enough to be planted outdoors.

There are several species of *Nerine* but only one, *N. bowdenii*, is hardy enough to live outdoors all the year round. The others can be stood outside in pots during the summer but need protection for the winter.

Any well drained soil is suitable but the best specimens are in a warm position so that they can finish flowering before the frosts come. The bulbs should be covered with moss or bracken during the winter to protect them from the worst of the weather. Although they resent being disturbed, the clumps should be lifted and split up in March if they become overcrowded.

49

Anemone, Geum, Bergenia

The bright red *Geum* 'Mrs Bradshaw' makes an excellent low plant for the front of borders where its arching flower stems stand well above the foliage in the late spring and summer.

Anemone coronaria
De Caen

Although the De Caen and St Brigid hybrid anemones are charming garden plants, it is really as cut flowers for the house that they excel. The multi-coloured flowers are shown off to perfection by the almost black centres.

Anemone coronaria
St. Brigid

Whereas the De Caen and St Brigid hybrids are the most colourful and spectacular of the spring flowering anemones, *Anemone blanda* is a charming little plant that flowers in February and early March. The true species is blue, but there are also white and pink varieties and one called *A.b. scythinica* which is white centred. *A. blanda* is particularly well suited to naturalizing and succeeds best in an open but not too sunny position. As with bulbs growing in grass, the foliage should not be mowed until it is dying.

The modern hybrid *Geum* plants are of mixed origin but are mainly derived from *G. chiloense* and *G. coccineum*. 'Mrs. Bradshaw' and 'Lady Stratheden' coming from the former. They have an average height of 60cm

Bergenia 'Ballawley'

Bergenia hybrids are very good ground-cover plants for large shrubberies; in March and April the thick evergreen leaves provide a good background to the pink or white flower-heads.

Bergenia 'Silberlicht'

and flower continually from May to September. Both are rather inclined to become straggly and are best if replaced every three years or so.

Bergenia cordifolia and its many varieties are extremely useful early flowering ground-cover plants. The large, leathery, evergreen leaves smother weeds admirably and provide a good background for the flowers. These appear during March and April and are carried about 60cm high. Good varieties include 'Admiral' (red), 'Baby Doll' (pink) and 'Bressingham White'. Although often relegated to semi-darkness among shrubs, these handsome plants deserve better treatment and are ideal for sunny banks where both the flowers and leaves develop their full colour. Old leaves should be removed periodically to prevent the plants becoming untidy.

51

Primula, Helleborus

Of the many spring-flowering *Primula* species, *P. juliae* 'Wanda' is among the earliest flowering and most welcome in the spring. It is similar to the primrose except that the flowers are bright purple with a yellow eye.

Helleborus foetidus and *H. corsicus* are both relations of the Christmas rose. The former shows its pale green, maroon-edged flowers in February with *H. corsicus* carrying its tall stems of many pale green flowers later in the spring. Both are evergreens.

The many different coloured hybrids of the primrose provide a welcome early splash of colour in the spring and, indeed, most of those bought as houseplants are quite hardy enough for outside. Although not strictly a primrose, *Primula juliae* 'Wanda' is one of the earliest flowering. Its bright purple flowers with a yellow eye are borne singly on 5cm stems and often appear in late February. Even better known is the multi-coloured polyanthus, modern hybrids of which are now available in pastel shades and even blue. They make lovely bedding plants as they flower at the same time as many of the best spring bulbs.

Helleborus corsicus

Helleborus foetidus

Relatives of the Christmas rose, *Helleborus niger*, are many and varied, one of the most commonly seen being the Lenten rose, *H. orientalis*. Although the true species is creamy white, one usually sees a mixture of colours from white to dark purple. The flowers are produced throughout the spring on 30–40cm tall stems. Another species often seen is *H. corsicus*. This is a taller plant, up to 60cm high, and is truly spectacular when it flowers during March and April. The flowers are borne in hanging clusters and are apple green with a faint purple rim. Both species are evergreen and succeed well in semi-shade, spreading freely from seed.

53

Astilbe, Dianthus, Lychnis, Anemone

Dianthus 'Mrs Sinkins'

Pinks and border carnations, *Dianthus* spp., are among the best-loved of our cultivated flowers. They flower all summer long.

In damp places or moist borders, the delicate red, pink or white flower-heads and deeply cut leaves of the *Astilbe × arendsii* hybrids really give of their best.

Dianthus 'Doris'

The modern *Astilbe* hybrids are a great improvement on the traditional species from which they come. Most are in flower from about June to August and their height varies from 50–90cm. Being for the most part sturdy, they seldom require supporting. The range of colours has been greatly extended in recent years and now varies from white and cream, to shades of pink and even bright red. Good varieties include 'White Gloria', 'Bressingham Beauty' (pink), 'Red Light' (brick red) and 'Fanal' (deep red). Damp conditions give the best results and, as such, astilbes make excellent plants for pool and stream margins.

Of the enormous *Dianthus* family, probably the most widely grown are the pinks and border carnations which have been cultivated for centuries. All are stocky or creeping plants with grass-like greyish foliage. The flowers range in colour from white, through pink, to

Lychnis chalcedonica also flowers in the summer. An intensely bright scarlet is the most usual colour but others are available.

Flowering in late summer and autumn, *Anemone hupehensis* hybrids in pink and white provide both height and charm to the borders.

bright red and often contain a mixture. Some of the best and most popular are the Allwoodii hybrids; these are partly derived from the old 'laced pinks' but are better in every respect, including the length of flowering season. Pinks like a sunny position and should be renewed from cuttings every three or four years to prevent them getting old and 'woody'.

Although *Lychnis chalcedonica* is another member of the *Dianthus* family, this is where any resemblance with carnations and pinks ends. It is essentially an herbaceous plant. The flower-heads appear from June to August and are the most striking scarlet; they are borne on stems up to 1m high. There is also a double-flowered form.

Anemone japonica is also listed as *A. hupehensis* and *A. hybrida*. It flowers from August to October, is about 45cm tall and is normally a delightful pale pink, though a white form does exist.

Paeonia, Papaver, Phlox

Paeonia lactiflora has cherry-pink flowers with cream and white centres.

The paeony, *Paeonia lactiflora* hybrids, are among the most spectacular of our herbaceous plants. In the early summer they grow into bold clumps with large double, semi-double and single flowers of white and every shade of red and pink.

If *Paeonia* have a fault, it is that they flower for rather a short time and are then over for another year; this period is for about two weeks in June. There are many hybrids, varying in colour from white and all shades of pink to bright red. Pink and white varieties also exist. Flowers may be single, semi-double or fully double. They are sturdy plants and staking is not needed. The flowers are borne well above the attractive foliage and are some 60–90cm high. They like a sunny position and resent disturbance.

The perennial or oriental poppy, *Papaver orientale*, has long been a garden favourite and, in many respects, resembles the paeony, particularly in size, sturdiness and colour. The flowering period is from late May to late June though some varieties manage a second flush in the autumn following a good summer. They vary in height

Herbaceous phlox, *Phlox paniculata* hybrids, are some of our most handsome border plants. They are tall and sturdy and come in white and every shade of pink.

Oriental poppies, *Papaver orientale* hybrids, have taken on a new look with the introduction of double, frilled and white varieties in addition to the traditional orange/scarlet.

from 60 to 90cm and in colour from bright red through flame to orange and even white. Nearly all have a black base to the petals. Propagation is best carried out using root cuttings.

The *Phlox* family is one of the most valuable for rockery and herbaceous plants; not only does it contain many species but these vary greatly in size and colour. *P. paniculata* is the most frequently grown herbaceous form and it also has the most varieties and hybrids; among the best are 'Cherry Pink' (bright carmine rose), 'Eva Cullum' (clear pink, red centre), 'Hampton Court' (almost blue), 'Starfire' (deep red) and 'White Admiral'. The heights vary from 75 to 100cm and all flower from July to September. *P. maculata* is also sometimes grown. Propagation of herbaceous *Phlox* is from root cuttings taken in March or April.

Sedum, Achillea, Geranium, Crocosmia

Herbaceous geraniums are available in a vast range of colours and vigour. They are mainly low-growing plants and are best near the front of borders. This is Geranium endressi 'Wargrave Pink'.

The taller growing *Sedum spectabile* hybrids provide a delightful change in the late summer and autumn. Their flat flower-heads are much loved by bees and butterflies.

Sedum spectabile is a valuable border plant. It has flat-topped flower-heads up to 45cm high that are at their best from August to October. 'Autumn Joy' is an exceptionally good variety with pink flowers. A sunny position is always preferred and the dead flower stems can be left to give interest through the winter and to protect the crown.

Achillea millefolium 'Cerise Queen' is a close relative of the weed 'yarrow' that infests our lawns. The true species has rather dirty white flowers but this cultivar is a delightful deep pink colour. It grows to 75cm tall and flowers from June to August. Another, and more familiar, species is *A. filipendulina* or golden plate. This is only suitable for large borders because it reaches 1.5–1.8m high. The broad, flat and compact flower-heads are golden yellow, appear in late June and are sometimes dried for winter decoration.

58

Crocosmia masonorum can only be described as an elegant plant. Its tall arching stems of bright orange flowers in the late summer are perfect for cutting.

Achillea millefolium

A. filipendulina

The grey furry leaves and bright cerise flower-heads of *Achillea millefolium* 'Cerise Queen' make a charming plant and a great contrast to the more familiar and much larger *A. filipendulina*.

Although one normally thinks of geraniums as bright red bedding plants that make such a glorious show in summer, those are really pelargoniums. The true *Geranium* species and hybrids are less showy but attractive plants in a wide range of colours from white and all shades of pink, lilac and purple to blue. They make excellent ground-cover plants and the herbaceous varieties may be anything from 30 to 90cm high. Some start flowering in May but the normal period is June to August or September.

The genus *Crocosmia* is often confused with *Montbretia* but is altogether finer in respect of size and showiness. Two modern varieties of *C. masonorum* are 'Vulcan' and 'Firebird', the former being slightly redder. Both grow to about 80cm high. Taller and even more spectacular is *C.* 'Lucifer'. All flower from early July until September.

Hemerocallis, Kniphofia,

Hemerocallis fulva hybrids come in many different shades of orange and pink and, although each flower only lasts a day, flowering continues from June to August.

Hemerocallis 'Chartreuse Magic'

Hemerocallis 'Pink Damask'

The day lily, *Hemerocallis fulva* hybrids, is a plant that has undergone vast improvements in recent years. The rather drab, dirty orange flower colour that used to be seen in so many gardens has given way to many more colours, including several shades of pink. The flowers are also larger and the flowering period is extended. Flowering carries on more or less continually from June to August, with the lily-like flowers being carried on stems 45–90cm high.

The modern 'red hot pokers' are derivatives of *Kniphofia uvaria*. They make tall plants with evergreen leaves some 90cm long, the stout flower stems rising to 1.5–1.8m on established specimens. Each flower stem carries many tightly packed, small tubular flowers. In the most widely grown varieties, these start red but, as they open, they turn brilliant orange. The plants remain in flower from June to August and, being natives of southern Africa, prefer a sunny position.

Rudbeckia, Gaillardia

The rather exotic looking red hot poker, *Kniphofia uvaria* hybrids, flowers in late summer. Varieties are available in many shades of orange and yellow.

*Gaillardia ×
grandiflora* is another plant useful for cutting throughout the summer. The flowers are of more than one colour, usually a combination of red and yellow.

Rudbeckia fulgida produces good flowers for cutting. The wiry stems support well the orange and brown flowers that appear with very dark centres in July.

The *Rudbeckia* family is made up of many species and hybridizing has led to the creation of a fine selection of varieties. They are characterized by their yellow, orange or brown daisy-shaped flowers with very pronounced and dark centres. The plants stand some 60–90cm high and are in flower in the late summer from August to October. The genus *Echinacea* is sometimes included with *Rudbeckia*.

The blanket flower, *Gaillardia aristata*, has been a favourite herbaceous plant for many years. The predominant colour is yellow but each flower also contains varying amounts of red in broad bands; the centre is usually dark brown. The height varies but is usually 60–90cm. The plant has a long flowering period that may last from June until the first autumn frosts. For the widest variety of flower colours and sizes, it should be grown from seed.

Acanthus, Delphinium,

Bear's breeches, *Acanthus mollis*, has imposing flower spikes and large, attractively cut leaves. It flowers from midsummer. The flowers can be dried for winter use.

The modern *Delphinium* hybrids are now available in every shade of blue and lilac together with white and pink. Their height makes them ideal for the back of borders.
They flower in early summer.

Acanthus mollis, bear's breeches, is something out of the ordinary. Both in and out of flower it is an attractive plant with deeply cut, large, shiny green leaves the design of which was much favoured by architects in ancient Greece. The flower stems last from June to August and are up to 1m tall, the top third being covered with closely packed lavender and white flowers. These have spiny bracts around them and may be dried for the winter.

Delphinium hybrids have long been garden favourites but they do need large borders to house them as the flower spikes can easily reach 1.5m high. The normal colour is blue but this may be in one of many shades and the centre of the flower is normally different to the rest. Modern breeding has resulted in white, lavender and purple flowers and there is now even a red one, though it is considerably less fine than the others.

The tall stems of *Scabiosa caucasica*, the perennial scabius, and its long flowering period (June to October) make it excellent for cutting. The composite flower-heads are of lilac, pale blue or white.

Echinops ritro is a tall plant with blue flower-heads in late summer each of which looks like a drumstick. A white variety also exists.

Delphiniums flower from June to August.

Echinops ritro, the globe thistle, is scarcely a thistle at all because it carries no spikes. It does, though, look like one and has enough height, up to 1m, to make it a plant for the rear of most borders. All parts are finely hairy, which gives the plant a greyish appearance. Blue is the normal flower colour but there is also a white variety.

One normally thinks of garden scabious as being an annual grown from seed but *Scabiosa caucasica* and its varieties is a perennial widely grown commercially as a cut flower. The largely blue flowers are borne on 60cm-high stems from June right through until September. 'Clive Greaves' is the normal and best variety. A red species, *S. rumelica*, is also grown but the flowers are considerably smaller.

Aquilegia, Iris, Lupinus

Aquilegia spp. and hybrids flower in early summer and are available in a wide range of mixed colours. The long-spurred hybrids, such as McKana's strain, are the best.

The columbines, or *Aquilegia* spp., are old favourites but modern hybrids hardly look the same plants as the varieties that were grown in the past. Each flower is of two different colours, the outer petals being one and the inner petals and spurs the other. Yellow, cream, pink, red and white are all found. The stems are some 60cm high, are sturdy enough to require no support, and bear flowers from June to August. McKana's Long Spurred hybrids are the best variety but other, shorter ones and with less prominent spurs are also grown.

The *Iris* family is so large and varied that we can only cover a select few here but certainly the most popular is the tall bearded iris, *I. germanica*. Named varieties of this have been available for many years and modern ones have a much wider colour range and larger flowers

Lupins are stately plants available
in virtually every colour
combination imaginable. They
flower in June and July.

than those of the past. All flower in June and vary in
height from 90 to 120cm. To maintain flower quality,
the clumps should be lifted and split up every three
years or so, preferably during August or September.

If any one plant is known to every gardener in the
country, it must surely be the lupin, *Lupinus* hybrids. Its
tall flower spikes reach 1m or more high and appear from
June to July in a wide range of colours. The individual
flowers are clustered together on the stem for up to half
its height and each consists of two colours or shades of
the same colour. The finest strain is definitely the Russell
hybrids. Unfortunately, the plants have rather a short,
albeit attractive, life and are best renewed every few years.
When a particular plant is favoured, propagation should
be by cuttings, but otherwise by seed.

Aster

Aster novi belgii 'Marie Ballard'

Aster novae angliae 'September Ruby'.

Aster amellus 'Brilliant'

The pride of the herbaceous border in the autumn is the Michaelmas daisy, *Aster novii belgii*, *A. novae angliae* and *A. amellus*. Modern varieties are less prone to mildew and flower from August to October in all shades of purple, lilac and pink.

Michaelmas daisies, *Aster* spp. have long been popular herbaceous plants and, today, we can find them in every shade of pink, blue, purple and almost red. Their height also varies greatly, from less than 30cm to over 1.2m. As a rule, they flower in September and October but some may start as early as July. The many daisy-like flowers, up to 5cm across, are carried on branched stems and provide a blaze of colour.

Until the introduction of the *A. novii belgii* and *A. novae angliae* species, mildew was a problem with all Michaelmas daisies; this is now a problem of the past. Like many herbaceous plants, they should be lifted and split up every three or four years; this is best done in November. Although the shorter varieties are sturdy, the taller ones will need supporting.

Helleborus

Although the Christmas rose, *Helleborus niger*, is an herbaceous plant, it is more at home among shrubs. They offer a fair degree of protection to the plant's pure white blooms that appear in the depths of winter and last for several weeks.

One of the few herbaceous plants that flower in the depths of winter is *Helleborus niger*, the Christmas rose. Its common name is rather optimistic, though, as it seldom flowers before the New Year without protection. The white flowers are some 10cm across and persist well into the spring. They are carried on stems up to 30cm high. As with most hellebores, the foliage is evergreen. *H. niger* resents being disturbed but can easily be propagated by sowing seed gathered soon after it is ripe. Semi-shade is preferred to full sun and the flowers look at their best when surrounded by a variety of evergreen shrubs and ground-cover plants.

Myosotis, Cheiranthus,

The wallflower is certainly the most popular plant for growing in formal bedding displays with tulips. In addition, the flowers have a delightful scent.

The forget-me-not, *Myosotis* spp., have long been favourite spring bedding plants for growing as under-plants with tulips or hyacinths.

There are several species of forget-me-not, *Myosotis*, but certainly the most widely grown is the biennial *M. alpestris*. The normal form is about 30cm but there is a dwarf form only half that height which is particularly attractive when grown in conjunction with yellow or pink hyacinths. The flowers of *Myosotis* are less than 1cm across and appear during April and May; they are the most beautiful sky blue in colour. Seed should be sown outdoors in May for flowering the following spring.

The wallflower, *Cheiranthus*, is beyond a doubt our most popular spring-flowering bedding plant. It is grown either as named varieties of one colour (e.g. Blood Red, Fire King, Ivory White, Cloth of Gold, Giant Pink) or as mixtures (Persian Carpet). The plants grow to about 45cm tall and are charmingly scented. Seed should be sown outdoors during May and the seedlings grown on in nursery rows until final planting out in October.

Viola, Primula

Although the main flowering time of pansies, *Viola* spp., is in the summer, there are several that flower early enough to be used for spring bedding.

Polyanthuses are not only excellent spring bedding plants, they can also be grown in pots for the house. The wide range of colours now includes blue.

Pansies, *Viola* spp., come in an enormous range of combination and single colours and, varying from 15 to 25cm tall, are especially popular as edging plants or for growing on their own in small borders or tubs. One kind or another will be found in flower virtually every month of the year. Pansies are an example of a hardy perennial that is normally grown for only one flowering season. Several strains will flower in the winter and early spring. They are available as mixtures, colour series and individual named varieties.

Polyanthus, *Primula* spp., flower throughout the spring. They are widely grown in formal bedding displays but are equally at home in shady borders among shrubs. They come in a wide range of colours including blue and pastel shades. Each flower stem is about 25cm high and is made up of some ten blooms. They are useful as cut flowers.

Begonia, Canna, Helichrysum,

There are two popular types of *Begonia*, tuberous rooted and fibrous rooted. The former are more often grown as pot plants and the latter for bedding.

Canna indica, Indian shot, gets its name from the bullet-like seeds. It is normally grown as a 'dot' plant for bedding displays where its large leaves and vivid orange flowers are a spectacular sight.

Fibrous rooted *Begonia* (half-hardy annuals) are popular summer bedding plants reaching about 15cm high. The flowers may be white or any shade of pink or red and the leaves green or almost brown. Their much taller and more showy relatives, the tuberous rooted begonias (half-hardy perennials), are normally grown as pot plants or among shorter bedding plants. Many flower shapes exist, including fully double and semi-double, and colours may be white, yellow, pink or red.

If not a particularly pretty plant, *Canna indica*, Indian Shot, is certainly colourful. The flowers are yellow, orange or red and the leaves green or brownish. It is used almost exclusively as a dot plant in formal summer bedding schemes. Although a half-hardy perennial, it is treated as an annual.

Some of the most popular flowers for drying for winter flower arrangements are those of the *Helichrysum* spp. (hardy annuals). The petals have a straw-like texture and

Matthiola

Ten-week stocks, *Matthiola* spp, have long been grown for their glorious scent, both in the garden and as cut flowers. They come in a range of colours from purple and red to pink and white.

Helichrysum spp. are grown almost exclusively for drying as winter decoration indoors. Their strawy petals come in a wide range of colours and retain their freshness for months.

retain their colour well. They come in a wide range from almost white, through pink, yellow and orange to wine red. The normal height of the plants is about 1m but a dwarf form exists which is only 30cm tall. For best results the stems should be picked when the flowers are just starting to open.

Some of the most strongly scented flowers in the garden are to be found among *Matthiola* spp., the stocks. White, and shades of pink and red, are the usual colours of the flower spikes, and individual flowers may be single or double. The plants vary in height from 30 to 60cm. Seven Week, Ten Week and Giant Excelsior stocks are half-hardy annuals, but the East Lothian and Brompton (winter-flowering) types are hardy biennials. Another variety, the Virginian or Night-scented stock, has single flowers, is rather straggly and is grown for its scent.

Pelargonium, Zinnia, Alyssum

The zinnia is a plant that thrives on sun and drought. The taller strains are excellent for cutting while the dwarf ones make good edging plants for borders.

Pelargonium zonale is not a geranium at all. It is treated solely as a half-hardy summer bedding plant where its glorious range of colours makes it one of the best of all.

Alyssum is one of the easiest and most widely grown formal dwarf bedding plants. Pure white is certainly the most popular colour, though others are available. It is often grown as an edging plant in combination with *Lobelia*.

The 'geranium' has long been a favourite summer bedding plant. Its correct name, however, is *Pelargonium zonale*. The flower colours are white and every imaginable shade of pink and red and the leaves may be pure green, green banded with brown or variegated green and white. The varieties used for bedding are normally about 60cm high but others may be as little as 25cm. Until recently, they could only be grown by taking cuttings in August and overwintering them. Now, though, there are strains that can be raised from seed each spring.

The various types of *Zinnia* (half-hardy annual) have long been known and grown for their brightness and showiness in the garden. They are especially valuable as cut flowers because of their lasting powers in water. Their size extends from the 15cm-high 'Thumbelina' right up to the 80cm Giant Double Flowered. The

flowers are double or semi-double and come in all shades of yellow, pink, orange, lavender and red, as well as white. The flowers of one species, *Z. mexicana*, are double and of several colours; it also withstands bad weather better than the others.

Alyssum maritimum (hardy annual) is probably as well known as any other flower but, as is so often the case, the name may not be familiar. The pure white cushions of flowers, frequently grown in conjunction with *Lobelia* as edging plants in formal borders, are a charming and common sight throughout the summer. It seldom exceeds 15cm high and the variety 'Minimum' is as little as 5cm. Pale rose-pink varieties are also grown. Another species, *A. saxatile*, is actually a perennial but is usually treated as an annual. It has a cascading habit and attractive golden-yellow flowers.

Nicotiana, Calendula, Eschscholtzia,

Nicotiana spp., tobacco plants, are popular plants for informal settings, mainly because of their glorious scent on warm summer evenings. They are available as single colours or mixed.

The marigold is another favourite and can now be had in a range of sizes and in all shades of orange and yellow.

The sweetly scented flowers of the tobacco plant, *Nicotiana* spp., have made it a firm favourite for many years. The scent is particularly noticeable on still, warm nights and when the plants are growing near a wall. The plants are mainly used in informal settings and vary in height from 25 to 100cm. The flowers are a very long trumpet shape and may be white or shades of yellow, pink or red; there is even a pale green variety, 'Lime Green'.

Although the history of the English marigold, *Calendula officinalis* (hardy annual), stretches way back in time, it is only recently that improved strains have been bred to extend the size and colour range. The flowers are 8–10cm across and may be fully- or semi-double. Their colour varies from pale yellow to deep orange. Plant size ranges from 25 to 60cm. They are hardy enough to be sown in the autumn to give, in the following year, a

Mimulus

The long flowering period and dwarf habit of *Eschscholtzia* spp. make them good informal bedding plants. The colours now include many shades of red and yellow as well as the original orange.

The multi-coloured flowers and low growth habit of *Mimulus* spp., monkey flowers, combine with their love of moisture to make them popular plants for damp places.

splash of colour in early summer.

Eschscholtzia spp. are normally known as the Californian poppies (hardy annuals). They are another example of plants that have undergone considerable improvement in recent years. The traditional colour of the single poppy-like flowers is bright orange but this has been extended to every shade of yellow, orange and pink and the flowers may now be semi-double. The plants reach about 30cm in height and will tolerate very poor soils.

The flower pattern of *Mimulus* spp. (half-hardy perennial) gave rise to their popular name of monkey flowers. Modern varieties, however, bear little resemblance to the originals as they are now found in every shade of yellow, orange, pink and red and are frequently spotted and marked with a second colour. All varieties are low growing and seldom exceed 23cm high. They are very useful for damp borders.

Antirrhinum, Dahlia, Lathyrus,

Named varieties of *Dahlia* are among the best cut flowers. They are normally grown from tubers but dwarf mixed strains can be grown from seed.

Snapdragons are popular bedding plants for both formal and informal settings. They are available in a wide range of sizes and colours.

Antirrhinum spp., snapdragons, are really hardy perennials but are treated as half-hardy annuals. They can be seen as named varieties containing one or more colours or as mixtures. Their height varies from 20 to 120cm with the most popular varieties about 60cm. The flowers are carried on a spike and may be of several different shapes, e.g. Penstemon flowered.

The traditional *Dahlia* (half-hardy perennial) is one of our most popular cut flowers. It has many flower forms, from the compact 'small poms' to the rather blousy 'large decoratives'. The plants can vary in height from 60cm to 1.5m and can be seen in most colours except green and blue. Dahlias can also be grown from seed sown each spring but these are grown more for their value as bedding plants than as cut flowers.

Sweet peas, *Lathyrus odoratus*, (hardy annuals) are, along with dahlias, cut flowers *par excellence*. They can be seen in every imaginable shade of pink, salmon, deep

Nemesia

Nemesia is a cheerful little half-hardy annual that is used for informal bedding.

Sweet peas also provide first-rate cut flowers, their glorious scent soon filling a room. There are now dwarf varieties that need no support.

scarlet, lilac and purple as well as white. They are self-clinging climbers and need the support of canes or netting when grown for cut flowers. Many, but not all, varieties are gloriously scented. There are now dwarf varieties that reach only 30–60cm in height, which is ideal for small borders; they not only supply cut flowers but are also very attractive plants in their own right.

Nemesia spp. (half-hardy annuals) are a riot of colour in the summer and autumn. They are excellent for small borders or as edging plants because the compact forms reach about only 23cm high and even the more vigorous *Nemesia strumosa* Suttoni are only 7–8cm more. Individual flowers are usually of more than one colour; these include shades of yellow, pink, orange and red.

Pansies have been dealt with as spring-flowering (see page 69), but there are summer-flowering types.

Tropaeolum, Lobelia, Campanula

Nasturtiums are available both as vigorous trailing plants and compact ones. They are very colourful and good for ground cover.

The main virtue of *Lobelia erinus* is its dwarf habit. Its colour range now includes near-red along with blue and white.

Canterbury bells are mainly tall-growing biennials with the characteristic blue bell-like flowers.

The actual height of nasturtiums, *Tropaeolum majus*, (half-hardy annual) is normally less than 30cm but this belies their vigour as the shoots of some varieties reach more than 1m in length. In complete contrast, there are compact ones that spread very little. The flowers are 7–8cm across and vary in colour from pale yellow to scarlet. One variety has marbled green and white leaves.

Probably the most popular edging plant is *Lobelia erinus* (half-hardy annual). Its colours include white and all shades of blue and there is now one that is almost red. 'Cambridge Blue' is a good light blue variety and 'Crystal Palace' one of the best dark blues. The habit of the plants is either compact, semi-spreading or trailing.

Canterbury Bells, *Campanula medium*, (hardy biennial) add valuable blue to borders early in the summer though, in fact, they can also be white or pink. Their height varies from 45 to 90cm. An unusual form is called 'Cup and Saucer', the flowers of which consist of a central trumpet and an outer ring of petals.

Chrysanthemum

For countless years chrysanthemums have held specialist gardeners in their spell but anyone can grow them with a little care. They are not only attractive and nicely scented but they last longer as cut flowers than most others. Korean chrysanthemums can even be grown as herbaceous plants.

Chrysanthemums, *Chrysanthemum* spp. and varieties, can be divided into disbudded varieties, which are restricted to one flower per stem, and spray varieties, which are allowed to develop many flowers per stem. They all flower naturally from autumn to early spring. Those varieties that flower before the autumn frosts may be grown out of doors but those flowering later are best grown in pots which should be brought under cover during September. The flower colours range from white, yellow, orange and red to pink and bronze. Besides the herbaceous 'Koreans', other species of chrysanthemum include 'Charm', which are grown in pots and are covered in a succession of small flowers, and 'Cascade', which are similar to Charm but have a trailing habit and are ideal for hanging baskets.

Pulsatilla, Saxifraga, Aubretia, Iris

Pulsatilla vulgaris has almost bell-like purple flowers in April filled with bright yellow stamens. These are followed by feathery seed-heads.

Aubrieta can be bought as named varieties or as mixed colours in purple, lilac and pink. They make ideal trailing plants for growing over walls and on terraces.

Pulsatilla vulgaris used to be called *Anemone pulsatilla* and this gives a good indication of its similarity to an anemone. Its flowers appear in April along with the feathery leaves and they last for about a month. They are followed by dandelion-like seed-heads which persist until the seeds ripen in the early summer. The plant attains a height of about 20cm.

The mossy saxifrages (*Saxifraga* dactyloides section) are true rockery plants that will form clumps of tightly packed moss-like shoots. During May, flower stems appear each carrying several small flowers. The stems grow some 15cm high and the flowers may be white or shades of pink or red. The vigour varies so the clumps can be 15–90cm across. Many different species are cultivated and there is a wealth of named varieties.

One of the most widely known rockery plants must be

The iris most suitable for the rockery is *I. pumila*. It flowers in May, is only a few centimetres high and produces normally deep purple flowers.

The mossy saxifrage species are perfect rock plants, their dwarf and compact growth soon spilling over the rocks. The flowers are carried well above the leaves.

Aubrieta deltoidea; there can be hardly a rockery in the country that has not got this trailing plant. The flowers appear during April and are beautifully shown off by the grey-green leaves. Their colour ranges from the palest lilac, through all shades of purple to a bright magenta. Seed sown in the spring is the normal method of propagation but named varieties are grown from cuttings.

Leaving aside the irises that grow from bulbs, *Iris pumila* is one of the earliest of this vast family to flower. Although each bloom lasts only a few days, an established clump may remain in flower throughout May. In shape, they are very like the common herbaceous Tall Bearded irises in miniature. They seldom reach more than 15cm in height and are usually different shades of purple but may also be pale blue or straw yellow.

Ajuga, Gentiana, Primula

Ajuga reptans has several different forms with a variety of attractively variegated leaves. 'Burgundy Glow' is one of the more vividly coloured kinds. Short spikes of blue flowers are produced from May to July.

The gentians are among the prettiest of rock plants. One of the best is *Gentiana verna* whose intense blue flowers appear on short stems in May and June.

The true (non-hybrid) *Ajuga reptans*, common name Bugle, is invasive and will quickly spread and smother any choicer plant too near it. It runs along the ground and even the flower-heads, which appear during May, are only some 7–8cm tall. More domesticated and less vigorous are the many variations that exist; those with purple/white and green/white variegated leaves are the prettiest. Although the weaker-growing varieties are safe in a rockery, Bugle is more often used as a ground-cover plant in shrub or herbaceous borders.

Gentians are some of the most beautiful and typically alpine plants that we grow. Possibly the best known is the spring flowering *Gentiana acaulis*. Its intensely blue trumpet-shaped flowers are about 5cm long and almost stemless. There is also a white form. *G. verna* is another classic with rather smaller and more open flowers borne

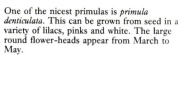

One of the nicest primulas is *primula denticulata*. This can be grown from seed in a variety of lilacs, pinks and white. The large round flower-heads appear from March to May.

Primula allionii

on 7–8cm long stems. Plants of this species should be renewed every three years or so; new ones can be raised from seed sown in the autumn.

Primula denticulata can be rather large for rockeries if on fertile soil but it makes a charming little plant if grown where the soil is poor. There are a host of other primulas that can be found in flower during the spring. One of the daintiest is *P. frondosa* (blooms in April), which has pale lilac flowers and leaves powdered with white. It barely reaches 10cm high. Another beauty, and particularly at home in a damp but sunny spot, is *P. rosea* 'Delight'. Though the leaves sometimes reach 15cm long, half that size is more normal with similar sized flower-heads. The flowers are an almost fluorescent pink. The variety 'Grandiflora' will do well in very moist, even boggy, soil.

Sempervivum, Helianthemum,

The houseleek is a strange-looking plant. A rather unusual species is *Sempervivum arachnoideum*. It has a small rosettes of fleshy, hairy leaves.

The dwarf, shrubby rockrose, *Helianthemum nummularium*, is a delight in June and July when the papery flowers appear. Yellow is the normal flower colour.

In many respects, the houseleek, *Sempervivum tectorum*, is one of the weirdest of garden plants but we are so familiar with its cactus-like appearance that most of us hardly give it a second glance. The true species has a tight rosette of largely green, fleshy leaves and sends up a 30cm-high reddish flower stem in June. The rosettes of *S*. 'Royal Ruby' are similarly sized but deep ruby red. *S*. 'Silverine' probably has the biggest rosettes of all, once established. They are pale silvery grey.

The shrubby rock rose, *Helianthemum*, is ideally suited to rockery conditions. It is low growing, rarely reaching more than 30cm. It has almost papery flowers throughout the summer and has so many named varieties of different colours that one is spoilt for choice. Among these are coppery gold, rosy red, flame, deep orange, yellow and even a red/white mixture called 'Raspberry Ripple'. The only real snag with *Helianthemum* is that

Sedum, Dianthus

The white to deep pink flowers of *Dianthus alpinus* make this dwarf pink a valuable rock plant.

Sedum spathulifolium has rosettes of thick, fleshy leaves. Its colour varies with the variety but, common to all, are the numerous stems of yellow flowers.

the plants get straggly after a few years if neglected so clipping after flowering is advisable.

Sedum is a large and variable genus; even for the rockery there are about a dozen suitable species. One of the most widely grown and accommodating is *S. spathulifolium capablanca*. This has small and close rosettes of pale grey leaves that contrast beautifully with the pale yellow flowers that appear in June. *S.s. purpureum* is similar but with purple leaves. *S. spurium* has a creeping, mat-forming habit.

The genus *Dianthus* has many species ideally suited to the drier conditions usually found in rockeries. *D. alpinus* is one of the best examples. It grows in glossy green cushions and has rose-pink flowers on very short stems in June and July. Most species grow to only 10cm high and are easily grown from seed. *Dianthus* spp. need replacing after a few years.

Phlox, Aethionema, Armeria, Thymus

Phlox douglasii is one of the best dwarf phloxes. Several varieties exist but they all flower from May to August in a range of colours from white to pink and crimson.

Aethionema 'Warley Rose' is a dwarf, semi-shrubby plant with small greyish-green leaves and heads of tiny bright pink flowers all summer long.

Some of the best varieties of *Phlox douglasii* are 'Daniels Cushion' (pink), 'Red Admiral' and 'May Snow'. All are in flower from late spring onwards and form tightly packed mounds up to 5cm high. Another good species is *P. subulata*. This also flowers in May and June. Good varieties include 'Apple Blossom' (pink), 'Oakington Blue Eyes' and 'Benita' (lavender). Both species like a sunny position and are propagated by cuttings taken after flowering.

The genus *Aethionema* comprises such small shrubs as hardly to warrant the name. Even the most vigorous of those suitable for rockeries, *A. pulchellum*, is only 25cm high while 'Warley Rose' is little more than 15cm. Both, however, make up for their smallness by being covered in bright pink flowers from May to July. The plants are only short lived but propagate readily from cuttings taken after flowering.

Though more associated with cliffs at the seaside,

One of the best thrifts is the miniature *Armeria caespitosa*. It is little more than 5cm high and carries small heads of lilac flowers.

Armeria maritima

thrift, *Armeria maritima*, makes a very good rockery plant. The tight cushions of thin leaves grow to a maximum of some 15cm high with the pink flower-heads a further 15cm above that. These last for about a month from late May. Several improved and named varieties exist including 'Alba' (white), and 'Dusseldorf Pride' (red).

The native wild thyme, *Thymus serphyllum*, has several improved varieties. All are good rockery plants forming tight mats of characteristically aromatic little leaves. The equally small flowers are borne in clusters; they are pink in the true species. 'Anderson's Gold' is especially dwarf, only 5cm high. It has bright yellow leaves that turn pale green with age. *T.s. coccineus* has the reddest flowers of all. Other good ones include *T. citriodorus aureus* (lemon scented, golden leaved, bushy) and 'Doone Valley' (leaves speckled with gold).

Hypericum, Achillea,

Hypericum olympicum is dwarf and spreading, the small grey leaves are evergreen and lemon yellow flowers are produced in profusion.

Achillea × *clavenae* × *lewisii* is a grand little plant with white flower-heads produced from June to October.

There are several dwarf shrubby hypericums. Besides *Hypericum olympicum*, one of the most commonly seen is *H. polyphyllum grandiflorum*. This reaches some 15cm in height and carries large golden flowers from June to August. *H.p. sulphureum* is the same but with lemon yellow flowers. Both have pale green, almost grey, foliage and are often grown on walls as well as in rockeries. Another popular species is the tiny and coppery green *H. reptans*. It flowers from June to September and is only 5cm tall.

All the achilleas suitable for rockeries are herbaceous. Their foliage is grey-green and they range form 10 to 20cm high. One of the smallest is *Achillea* 'King Edward'; it is 10cm tall, with primrose-yellow flower-heads from June to August. At 12cm, *A. argentea* is slightly taller with silvery foliage and white flowers.

Cerastium, Campanula

Cerastium tomentosum, snow-in-summer, is a ground-cover plant *par excellence*. Its grey-leaved stems spread quickly and it has dainty white flowers. It is much too vigorous for small rockeries.

Campanula carpatica has many sub-species and varieties, all of which are good rockery plants. They flower from June to August and vary from shades of blue to lilac and white.

Cerastium tomentosum is scarcely a rockery plant. It is, though, unsurpassed for ground-cover and will quickly spread to conceal any undesirable feature on the ground. A much neater species and perfectly safe for even a small rockery is *C. columnae*. This has the characteristic grey foliage and white flowers in June and July but lacks the rampant, spreading habit.

Those varieties of *Campanula carpatica* most commonly grown include *C.c.* 'Blue Moonlight' (light blue, 25cm high), 'Bressingham White' (25cm) and 'Hannah' (white, 15cm). Equally suitable for rockeries and somewhat smaller are the varieties of *C. cochlearifolia*.

Glossary

Annuals   Plants that grow, flower and die in a single year, e.g. marigold.

Biennials   Plants that grow one year, flower in the next and then die, e.g. sweet william.

Bract   A reduced leaf that often appears close to flowers.

Climbers   Plants which scramble up walls, fences or taller plants with or without aid from the gardener.

Conifers   Fir trees.

Deciduous   A tree or shrub whose leaves are shed each autumn.

Disbud   Normally, to remove all but the topmost flower or growth bud from a stem.

Double flower   Having so many petals that a true centre to the flower is hard to see.

Evergreen   A tree or shrub whose leaves are retained all-year-round.

Flower-head   A number of flowers borne in a cluster or group on a single stem, e.g. michaelmas daisy.

Flower spike   A flowering stem with closely packed flowers, e.g. lupin and delphinium.

Formal   Plants grouped together to form strict lines and/or patterns.

Ground cover   Creeping plants which hug the ground and seldom grow to any appreciable height.

Half-hardy	Likely to be damaged by even a slight frost.
Hardy	Having the ability to withstand normal amounts of frost.
Herbaceous plant	Normally one which dies back to the ground each autumn but reappears in the spring, e.g. paeony.
Informal	Plants grouped together to give a more or less natural appearance.
Hips	The seed capsules of roses.
Leggy	Having unnaturally long stems largely devoid of side-shoots and leaves.
Organic matter	Any soil additive of animal or vegetable origin but usually referring to garden compost, farmyard manure or peat.
Perennials	Herbaceous plants that grow and flower each year for many years, e.g. lupins.
Raceme	An arrangement of flowers similar to a spike but pendulous, e.g. *Wisteria*.
Reflexed	Bent backwards; as with petals.
Semi-double flower	Having a large number of petals but also a distinct centre to the flower, e.g. *Calendula*.
Sequestrene	Plant foods in a form that will remain available in a chalky or limey soil.
Single flower	Having a single row or petals around the centre of a flower, e.g. primrose.
Variegated	Of more than one colour. Usually refers to leaves.

Index

93

Acknowledgements

Artwork © Newnes Books, a Division of The Hamlyn Publishing Group Limited. Artists: Tim Hayward – Linden Artists, Pat Harby – Linden Artists, Stephen Kirk – The Hayward Art Group, Cynthia Pow, Kristin Rosenberg H.R.M.S., Charles Stitt. Cover: Cynthia Pow.

Photographs A–Z Botanical 26, 30, 35, 36, 73, 77; R & C Foord 55; Newnes Books, Adrian Davies 29, Peter Loughran 87; NHPA, G. E. Hyde 62; The Harry Smith Horticultural Photographic Collection 17, 23, 65, 67, 71, 74, 81, 83; Charles Stitt 41, 56, 69, 79. Cover: Robert Pearson.